## DEBORAH BRUCE

Deborah Bruce is a playwright and theatre director. Her other plays include *Godchild* at Hampstead Theatre, *Same* for the National Theatre Connections Festival 2014, *The Distance* at the Orange Tree Theatre and Sheffield Crucible, *The House They Grew Up In* at Chichester Festival Theatre, *Joanne* for Clean Break at Soho Theatre and *Guidesky and I* at the Orange Tree Theatre. *The Distance* was a finalist for the 2012-13 Susan Smith Blackburn Prize.

**Other Titles in this Series**

Mike Bartlett
ALBION
BULL
GAME
AN INTERVENTION
KING CHARLES III
SNOWFLAKE
VASSA *after* Gorky
WILD

Deborah Bruce
THE DISTANCE
GODCHILD
THE HOUSE THEY GREW UP IN
SAME

Jez Butterworth
THE FERRYMAN
JERUSALEM
JEZ BUTTERWORTH PLAYS: ONE
MOJO
THE NIGHT HERON
PARLOUR SONG
THE RIVER
THE WINTERLING

Caryl Churchill
BLUE HEART
CHURCHILL PLAYS: THREE
CHURCHILL PLAYS: FOUR
CHURCHILL PLAYS: FIVE
CHURCHILL: SHORTS
CLOUD NINE
DING DONG THE WICKED
A DREAM PLAY *after* Strindberg
DRUNK ENOUGH TO SAY I LOVE YOU?
ESCAPED ALONE
FAR AWAY
GLASS. KILL. BLUEBEARD'S FRIENDS.
    IMP.
HERE WE GO
HOTEL
ICECREAM
LIGHT SHINING IN BUCKINGHAMSHIRE
LOVE AND INFORMATION
MAD FOREST
A NUMBER
PIGS AND DOGS
SEVEN JEWISH CHILDREN
THE SKRIKER
THIS IS A CHAIR
THYESTES *after* Seneca
TRAPS

debbie tucker green
BORN BAD
DEBBIE TUCKER GREEN PLAYS: ONE
DIRTY BUTTERFLY
EAR FOR EYE
HANG
NUT
A PROFOUNDLY AFFECTIONATE,
    PASSIONATE DEVOTION TO
    SOMEONE (– *NOUN*)
RANDOM
STONING MARY
TRADE & GENERATIONS
TRUTH AND RECONCILIATION

Arinzé Kene
GOD'S PROPERTY
GOOD DOG
LITTLE BABY JESUS & ESTATE WALLS
MISTY

Lucy Kirkwood
BEAUTY AND THE BEAST
    *with* Katie Mitchell
BLOODY WIMMIN
THE CHILDREN
CHIMERICA
HEDDA *after* Ibsen
IT FELT EMPTY WHEN THE HEART
WENT AT FIRST BUT IT IS ALRIGHT NOW
LUCY KIRKWOOD PLAYS: ONE
MOSQUITOES
NSFW
TINDERBOX
THE WELKIN

Chinonyerem Odimba
AMONGST THE REEDS
PRINCESS & THE HUSTLER
UNKNOWN RIVERS

Luke Norris
GOODBYE TO ALL THAT
GROWTH
SO HERE WE ARE

Bijan Sheibani
THE ARRIVAL

Stef Smith
ENOUGH
GIRL IN THE MACHINE
HUMAN ANIMALS
NORA : A DOLL'S HOUSE *after* Ibsen
REMOTE
SWALLOW

Jack Thorne
2ND MAY 1997
BUNNY
BURYING YOUR BROTHER IN
THE PAVEMENT
A CHRISTMAS CAROL *after* Dickens
THE END OF HISTORY...
HOPE
JACK THORNE PLAYS: ONE
JUNKYARD
LET THE RIGHT ONE IN
    *after* John Ajvide Lindqvist
MYDIDAE
THE SOLID LIFE OF SUGAR WATER
STACY & FANNY AND FAGGOT
WHEN YOU CURE ME
WOYZECK *after* Büchner

Phoebe Waller-Bridge
FLEABAG

The Wardrobe Ensemble
1972: THE FUTURE OF SEX
EDUCATION, EDUCATION, EDUCATION
THE LAST OF THE PELICAN
    DAUGHTERS

Joe White
MAYFLY

Deborah Bruce

# RAYA

NICK HERN BOOKS
London
www.nickhernbooks.co.uk

**A Nick Hern Book**

*Raya* first published in Great Britain as a paperback original in 2021 by Nick Hern Books Limited, The Glasshouse, 49a Goldhawk Road, London W12 8QP

*Raya* copyright © 2021 Deborah Bruce

Deborah Bruce has asserted her right to be identified as the author of this work

Cover photograph by Freddie Woodward Images

Designed and typeset by Nick Hern Books, London
Printed in Great Britain by Mimeo Ltd, Huntingdon, Cambridgeshire PE29 6XX

A CIP catalogue record for this book is available from the British Library

ISBN 978 1 83904 006 1

Woodland
CARBON
www.woodlandcarbon.co.uk
NICK HERN BOOKS
Printed on Carbon Captured paper

*Raya* was first performed at Hampstead Theatre Downstairs, London, on 11 June 2021. The cast was as follows:

| | |
|---|---|
| ALANNAH | Shannon Hayes |
| JASON | Bo Poraj |
| ALEX | Claire Price |
| GRACE | Elena Coleman/Ruby Woolfenden |

| | |
|---|---|
| *Director* | Roxana Silbert |
| *Designer* | Moi Tran |
| *Design Associate* | Mona Camille |
| *Lighting Designer* | Matt Haskins |
| *Sound Designer and Composer* | Nick Powell |

## Characters

ALEX, *forty-nine*
JASON, *forty-nine*
ALANNAH, *nineteen*
GRACE, *ten*

## Notes on the Play

A dash (–) indicates an abrupt interruption.

A forward slash (/) in the middle or at the end of a line denotes an overlap in dialogue.

… indicates a trailing off.

*This text went to press before the end of rehearsals and so may differ slightly from the play as performed.*

*Night.*

*A city outside London.*

*A student house. An empty front room.*

*A car pulls up outside.*

*Muffled voices, the sound of a key in the lock and the front door opens straight into the front room.*

*A man and woman enter bringing light from the street.*

*The woman is* ALEX, *she's 49. She steps inside.*

ALEX. Okay. Wow.

*The man is* JASON, *he's 49 too. He reaches for the light switch but no light comes on.*

JASON. Oh.

*He switches the switch on and off, no light.*

ALEX. Wow.

JASON. Hang on, what? What's wrong with the?

ALEX. Is there meant to be electricity?

JASON. Is there *meant* to be?

ALEX (*laughing*).

JASON. Er, yes. It's a fully functioning house. I rent it out with electricity thrown in.

*He closes the front door behind them and turns on the torch on his phone.*

*He illuminates a corner of the room and the door into the hall.*

Stay there a second.

JASON *makes his way through the room and into the hall.*

ALEX *stands by the front door.*

ALEX (*calls*). Do you know what, Jase, it still smells exactly the same. It's like, I don't know what, it's kind of like peaches and gas.

JASON (*off*). Gas? Don't say that.

ALEX. Not gas, it's a peachy gas smell, sweet like peaches as well.

JASON (*off*). Yum.

ALEX. Like peach air freshener or something. / Exactly the same.

JASON (*off*). Right. I'm taking the bulb out of a lamp.

ALEX. How can a place smell the same for thirty years, what makes smell?

JASON (*off*). Actually I'm just gonna unplug this lamp and bring it through there.

JASON *appears with a lamp.*

*He bangs into the door.*

*He uses his phone torch to find the plug socket and huffing and puffing in his coat he plugs in the lamp and switches it on.*

*There's light.*

Still a bit dark but.

JASON *re-angles the light.*

ALEX. No, dark's good.

JASON. 'Is there meant to be electricity?' What do you think this is, a mud hut!

ALEX *laughs.*

What kind of landlord would I be –

ALEX *laughs*.

ALEX. I just meant because it's empty, / perhaps it's been switched off –

JASON. Hold on, I'm just off to the well for water.

ALEX *laughs*.

I can't offer you anything I'm afraid.

ALEX. I stole the wine!

JASON. You stole the wine! Of course.

JASON *goes out into the hall and through to the kitchen*.

I'll get a couple of rocks chiselled into the shape of a drinking vessel.

*A light comes on in the kitchen, it bleeds through.*

ALEX *laughs loudly so it carries into the kitchen*.

ALEX *takes a bottle of wine out of her coat pocket*.

*She's nervous, a bit stressed. Changes her parting in the mirror.*

ALEX *(calls)*. Get mugs!

JASON *(off)*. Mugs?

ALEX. Yes, we always drank wine out of mugs.

JASON *(off)*. We have glasses. Wouldn't you rather have a glass?

ALEX. No! Let's do it properly. I want to feel what it's like to be a student again.

ALEX *takes off her coat and throws it onto the arm of the chair*.

*She changes her parting back how it was in the mirror.*

*She leaves the room.*

Can I look around?

JASON (*off*). Feel free.

ALEX (*off*). Can I look upstairs?

JASON (*off*). Go for it.

ALEX (*off*). Oh my god the super-steep stairs.

JASON *comes back into the front room with wine glasses.*

JASON *takes off his coat. He checks his phone. We can hear* ALEX *moving around upstairs.*

ALEX *comes back in.*

ALEX. It's so strange.

JASON. I've taken an executive decision on the mugs.

ALEX. Aww, spoilsport.

JASON. If you're sophisticated like me, once you've drunk wine from a glass there's no going back.

ALEX. Am I overruled?

JASON. You are.

JASON *opens the wine.*

ALEX. I don't remember knowing that you owned the house, / did I, I don't think I did

JASON. Well my parents owned the house –

ALEX. And then they gave it to you?

JASON. I bought it off them, yeh. In 1997 –

ALEX. I feel like I've tipped backwards in time.

JASON. You didn't come here a lot, did you?

ALEX. Yes I did, you know I did!

JASON. I remember maybe a couple of times.

ALEX. JASON!

JASON. Really?

ALEX. Come on, don't be shy!

JASON. You've got a better memory than me!

ALEX. Bit offensive

JASON. I'm joking

I didn't think you'd want to be reminded necessarily /

ALEX. I don't need to be reminded, unlike some people!

JASON. Of course I remember!

ALEX. We had a good time.

JASON. We did. / Shall we leave it at that?

ALEX. I can say that, can't I?

JASON. Of course, say what you like. Have some wine.

ALEX. 'Shut up and have some wine, Alex.'

JASON. Enough talking, drink!

*They drink wine.*

*They look at each other.*

ALEX. What?

JASON. Nothing.

*He raises his glass to her.*

Cheers

ALEX. Cheers! To what?

JASON. Being young and carefree and knowing nothing of the heartache to come.

ALEX. That's a bit dark!

JASON. I know! I don't know where that came from.

ALEX. Cheers! To young bodies and loads of sex!

JASON. Okay.

ALEX. Can you go with that?

JASON. Okay! Young bodies!

*They clink glasses.*

*They drink.*

ALEX. It sounds a bit pervy when you say it.

JASON. I know, let's move on

ALEX. Don't worry I'm going to call a cab after this.

JASON. Thank God.

ALEX. I just wanted to see the house.

JASON. It's the same, we haven't done anything to it. Just freshened it up between tenants.

ALEX. Yeh, so where are the tenants?

JASON. I'm selling it, it's too much work, I can't be. My wife – dealt with it.

ALEX. My wife, you keep saying my wife.

JASON. Do I?

ALEX. Yes!

JASON. Okay!

*They drink.*

ALEX. So. What does she do, your wife?

JASON. She. She's a therapist.

ALEX. Oh okay, that's /

JASON. Yeh! /

ALEX. Handy. To have, in-house.

JASON. Yes. So she had more –

ALEX. Patience

JASON. I was going to say time, but yes that as well.

There's a house in Suffolk that we Airbnb some of the year as well so it's a lot of, / too much work really, now.

ALEX. Okay!

Wow.

JASON *looks around the room.*

JASON. Sorry, I forgot half the furniture's gone, it's not very –

ALEX. We can sit on the floor!

JASON. I should be thinking about clearing the rest of this stuff out, and the kitchen, I haven't really thought all that through, that's boring –

ALEX. And your girls are what? Ten and fourteen?

JASON. Ten and fifteen, yes, nearly spot on.

ALEX. I'm a Facebook spy.

JASON. You're not are you! I don't go on it much.

ALEX. All the running! The marathon!

JASON. Triathalon –

ALEX. I didn't get round to donating / on the page

JASON. Don't worry, no pressure, we hit the target and then some.

ALEX. Such beautiful birthday cakes!

JASON. Yes, we love cake.

*Pause.* JASON *nodding.*

ALEX. Sorry I said 'young bodies, loads of sex'. It's ringing in my ears, it was stupid.

JASON. No problem.

ALEX. I wasn't trying to – I've got a hotel.

JASON. I know.

ALEX. It was probably, it's inappropriate, / I'm a bit

JASON. No it was funny.

ALEX. giddy. I'm overwhelmed or something. After seeing all those old people!

JASON. The old fat baldies?

ALEX. When the barman pointed to the cordoned-off area I was like, who are all these *old* people at our reunion?

JASON. No wonder they cordoned us off! Putting up big screens –

ALEX. Everyone's a version of someone you recognise, but sturdier. / Ruddier.

JASON. I think there's an app you can get that does that!

ALEX. I don't know what I expected,

JASON. We must be around thirty or forty stone heavier I reckon – as a year group

ALEX. None of us stay the same, do we?

JASON. Except you do look the same.

ALEX. Don't lie! I saw your face, who the hell's that?

JASON. No, actually.

ALEX. Alright maybe, she's *vaguely* familiar

JASON. I saw you before you saw me!

ALEX. Did you?

JASON. Yeh. When you walked in.

ALEX. Were you going to come over or –

JASON. Of course!

ALEX. I hardly knew anyone there.

    *Pause.*

JASON. I'm impressed you came by yourself.

ALEX. I just thought fuck it.

JASON. Good for you /

ALEX. And I'm in the middle of a project so – it means I've got an extra-heavy bag but I brought my camera, a couple of lenses, I can kill two birds /

JASON. Chuck your camera at them /

ALEX. Yeh! Get a couple of images if I'm lucky /

JASON. Great! I was going to ask if you were still into photography – / what's the project –

ALEX. Yes, keeping my hand in. Oh I'm just working on a small series of images around – it's early days, around the site of a fatality? You know where there's been a fatality? / Where you see the flowers and candles left by friends and relatives

JASON. Oh right.

ALEX. Yes. Car accidents – or y'know, the ghost bikes. Also shootings – stabbings. That type of thing. Yeh, I'm taking photographs of those sites. For a project. Called Flowers Left At The Scene.

JASON. Okay!

ALEX. Bit morbid but –

JASON. Yeh. I was going to say! Whoa!

*Pause.*

Really, great though. / Thought provoking.

ALEX. Thanks. It's been really good to be working creatively on something –

JASON. I'd be interested to see that – when it's finished.

ALEX. Because I've been having a bit of a bad time recently, so

JASON. Oh –

ALEX. But tell me more about all your great stuff!

JASON. I'm sorry to hear that /

ALEX. Your girls are *stunning*, oh my God!

JASON. Thank you, yeh they're / great

ALEX. And obviously work-wise, all good, I mean you must
be – you have lots of travel, you travel all over the place –
how's. I don't know, how's work?

ALEX *is crying, trying to hide it.*

JASON. Oh. Are you – ?

ALEX. No, no, don't! This happens all the time, nothing! Tell
me about, do you know what, this is a terrible thing to admit
but I don't really understand what it is you do –

JASON. Oh, right.

ALEX. What are you, a gigolo?

JASON. Sadly not, no. It's just a boring, so – Me and a couple
of guys, Phil was one of them actually, he was there tonight
– in a pinky-orange shirt – / we set up a business consulting
company

ALEX. That was *Phil*?

JASON. a software development, web design, online booking
systems, moving into franchise developing and marketing in
the early two thousands /

ALEX. Now all I can hear is blahblahblah!

JASON. I warned you – it's dull!

ALEX. I'm joking – go on

JASON. Well – we rode the wave of the internet in the nineties
basically, we struck lucky with timing, an explosion of start-
ups, small businesses, their success became our success –
that's it really.

Do you want a tissue or –

ALEX. Actually a tissue would be, thanks.

JASON *gets up and goes to his coat pockets but there's
nothing suitable, so he waves towards the door and leaves
the room.*

Oh no don't worry!

JASON. I'll just get some –

JASON *exits*.

ALEX *waits, she speaks under her breath*.

ALEX. For fuck's sake what the hell are you *doing*, you stupid arsehole idiot are you fucking Off Your Head, what the *hell*? Get it together.

JASON *re-enters with toilet roll*.

ALEX *has got it together*.

JASON. Not very glamorous, there you go.

ALEX. Thank you. (*Blows her nose*.)

JASON *stays standing in the doorway listening up the stairs*.

JASON. Did you hear that?

ALEX. No.

*Silence. They listen.*

ALEX. What was it?

JASON. It was like a squeal, or a

ALEX. A squirrel?

JASON. A squeal

*They listen.*

ALEX. Do you think it's a ghost?

JASON. It sounded like a pig –

ALEX. Do you think it's a *pig*?

JASON. No, it's more likely to be a ghost, you're right.

ALEX. It probably is literally more likely to be a ghost!

JASON. Except ghosts don't exist, and pigs do, / we could probably get the stats on this.

ALEX. Ghosts exist!

*They listen.*

JASON. I don't think it's anything.

ALEX. It's the ghost of our younger selves.

JASON. That'll be it.

JASON *comes back into the room and sits down.*

Are you all right now?

ALEX. So. Your company's doing really well then is it, obviously it is, all the holidays

JASON. Actually I sold it. Yeh, I cut loose, I made a good, it left me in a good position /

ALEX. As in you never have to work again?

JASON. I don't know about that.

ALEX. Oh my God, you've *retired*?

JASON. I'm still on the board / but

ALEX. How *old* are we?

JASON. Well, I retired young!

ALEX. Wow, you've done well!

JASON. The timing was lucky –

ALEX. Come on, well done.

JASON. Well, it wasn't bad /

ALEX. A man of leisure! Are you a member of a gentleman's club?

JASON. I am actually, a sort of low-key one

ALEX. Brandy and cigars

JASON. More herbal teas really

ALEX. Do they let women in?

JASON. For the lap dances obviously

ALEX. The lapsang dances?

JASON. Very good.

*Pause.*

What happened there? (*Indicating the tissue.*)

ALEX. Yeh yeh, it's just a hormonal thing, I'm having, at the moment, it's not a real, y'know.

JASON. Right – nothing I said then?

ALEX. No, of course not!

JASON. Okay, good.

ALEX. Yeah I'm really upset you sold your special franchise business company!

JASON. Sorry about that –

ALEX. And I wanted my wine in a mug!

JASON. Shit, I knew that would come back to bite me.

*They laugh.*

ALEX. Wow.

Being here!

*They hold eye contact for a moment. ALEX looks away.*

So. What now? Do I call a cab, or?

JASON. It's up to you.

ALEX. Should I stay the night? For old time's sake blah blah.

JASON. Oh!

Right!

ALEX. Is that too much? I can't read you. Sorry, have I gone too far?

JASON. You're married, right?

ALEX. *You're* married, right?

JASON. *Are* you married?

ALEX. Yes I am, I'm just wondering whether – if I stayed the night, maybe that wouldn't really be about that.

JASON. Okaaay

ALEX. I thought, y'know, thirty years ago, we used to, well, you've forgotten all about it, we've established that!

JASON. No / no I haven't.

ALEX. Okay so, would it be so terrible, I don't know. Maybe, I've misjudged this, have I? I thought, when we were talking at the pub, there was a fizz?

JASON. Yeh, I mean –

ALEX. A remnant of – And in the cab?

JASON. A remnant? I don't know. My wife –

ALEX. 'My wife' –

JASON. So what's going on in your relationship then, tell me about that –

ALEX. What do you need to know, about it?

JASON. Well, is it an open relationship?

ALEX. It's not open, no it's not –

JASON. Okay –

ALEX. There is a gap, I suppose, recently there's been, a slight gap's opened up, between us, to a certain.

Forget it.

JASON. A gap.

ALEX. Well, a crack, it's more a crack /

JASON. Is he a structural engineer?

ALEX. Look, sorry I cried, that's made it all. / Less sexy, hasn't it.

JASON. No, I'm just wondering what's going on / for you –

ALEX. Less Sexy, they should have booked that band to play at the reunion!

JASON. You know, I thought we were just talking –

ALEX. Anyway, crying wasn't part of the plan.

JASON. You had a plan?

ALEX. Forget it. I should probably head back to my hotel in a bit, what do you think?

JASON. I didn't know there was a plan, what's the plan?

ALEX. Look. I was excited about seeing you again, that's all.

When I saw on the Facebook group that you were one of the organisers.

I found myself wondering what it would be like to, see you.

I thought about how our relationship had been.

I looked through the pictures on your Facebook page and –

Wondered if this was an / opportunity to – maybe –

JASON. Those pictures are – really old.

ALEX. I shouldn't have invited myself back here, I just invited myself basically, didn't I?

JASON. No, you're good. / It's fine

ALEX. Okay good. Good!

JASON. But.

Yeah.

Maybe you coming back here wasn't the most sensible idea.

ALEX. Oh really? / Okay.

JASON. Sorry.

ALEX. No, fair enough, of course, your *wife*.

JASON. Yeh. I just think, all things considered, it would be better –

ALEX. If I called a cab. Fine. I'm going to do that now.

JASON. Okay. Thanks.

ALEX *stands up and puts on her coat.*

Thanks, Alex.

ALEX. Okay!

JASON. Actually, hey let *me* sort the cab

ALEX. Wow! I don't think anyone has ever been this grateful to me for going away!

JASON. What? No!

JASON *gets up and looks for his phone.*

ALEX *stands, gathers her stuff, and then waits awkwardly.*

ALEX. Okay, so this is horrible. You literally cannot wait to get rid of me /

JASON. Listen, let's, do you want to hook up back in London?

ALEX. At your gentleman's club? What for?

JASON. Old times' sake, catch up properly

ALEX. *This* is for old times' sake, this is that very moment. That's what this *is*.

I don't need a catch-up in London with some guy I used to have sex with at uni.

JASON. No I mean as a friend, a friend's catch-up

ALEX. I don't need a friend.

JASON. Well hey, I do!

Look, I'm going to give you my number

ALEX. What do you need a friend for, / you've got loads of friends

JASON. Here, I'm going to AirDrop you my contact details

ALEX. You knew every single person there, Phil and –

Really. I don't want your number

*Her phone beeps.*

JASON. There you go.

ALEX. How did you do that?

JASON. I just clicked on your –

ALEX. Well, that's creepy

It's like my phone's been raped.

JASON. That's a bit strong. What's your hotel?

ALEX. Don't worry about it, I'll walk

JASON. Don't be daft, I'm getting you a cab

ALEX. I'd rather walk

JASON. Don't be like that, what are you being like that for?

ALEX. It's fine, I understand, you don't want to talk about it because it makes you feel insecure.

JASON. Talk about what?

ALEX. You and me, in this house.

JASON. What?

ALEX. Maybe it's easier for your ego to just pretend you don't remember, maybe you've even pretended to yourself, protected yourself, you've blanked me out.

JASON. I don't know what you're, what are you saying?

ALEX. You know what I'm saying. You'd tried to have sex with that girl in Lanzarote when you were fifteen on a family holiday, on a roof or something, and you hadn't been able to manage it, her English was bad, you couldn't communicate, you were embarrassed and, ran away /

JASON. Whoa!

ALEX. The next day you were in a bar on the beach with your parents and the girl came in with her friends. They sat at the next table and laughed at you and flicked their milkshake at you and it landed on the back of your neck /

JASON. *What?* What the *hell*?

ALEX. They were flicking it at you, it was obvious they were pretending it was sperm /

JASON. Stop! How do you remember that!

ALEX. You were mortified! Your parents were there! Years passed and by the time you came here, you were completely locked in /

JASON. Locked in, what the!

ALEX. Sexually. Uptight, obviously understandably, paranoid, fearful, freaking out about being a virgin in your second year at uni, / come on, give me some credit!

JASON. Not a *virgin*, / credit for what?

ALEX. Yes you were. I sorted you out! I helped you out, didn't I?

JASON. What the hell?

ALEX. I healed you, *transformed* you!

JASON. Hold on

ALEX. I built you back up, I gave you confidence, didn't I? Well, you said I did.

JASON. I have absolutely no memory of telling you that, or having conversations about any of this /

ALEX. You used to say it. We talked about it, you told me /

JASON. Are you sure you've got the right guy here?

ALEX. Errr, yes!

JASON. Why would you remember some, irrelevant stupid story about a milkshake, / on *my* family holiday –

ALEX. It wasn't irrelevant, it was who you were! It defined you, no one could get near you.

JASON. Okay. Well, I suppose I don't remember it like that –

ALEX. It was the whole foundation of our relationship, me, guiding you out of that place

JASON. Whaat? I don't even remember us as *having* a relationship, I was just, maybe once or twice after a party or whatever, we'd come back here, I don't remember it being that big a deal

ALEX. Okay, wow.

JASON. I'm not being rude.

ALEX. I mean it really was a big deal. For you I mean, not so much for me.

JASON. I *remember* you obviously

ALEX. Well, *good*

JASON. I mean it clearly *was* a big deal for you though /

ALEX. No, no, it was *not* a big deal for me, it was just a side-thing for me,

I was actually seeing someone else, / other people,

JASON. I remember you as someone really fun, y'know confident, easygoing

ALEX. Yeh I was, that's right! That was me! But not you.

JASON. So what's weird, is that it's *you* that's held on to this

ALEX (*pause*). Okay.

JASON. I just mean, I'm not being rude, but I really haven't thought of you since, that time. Not being rude.

ALEX. Okay, well, *that's* what's weird, bearing in mind y'know, but that's fine –

JASON. And you remember stupid stuff about some idiot girl on a holiday I had when I was fifteen which I don't even –

ALEX *smiles, nods.*

Do you know what I mean? I don't even remember
mentioning anything about that, or thinking anything
about it –

ALEX. Well, it definitely was a big deal for you at the time –

JASON. I certainly haven't thought about it since

ALEX. Well neither have I, obviously

JASON. Well, you obviously have, so –

ALEX. Only in relation to seeing you tonight. Thinking in
retrospect about how much you owe me! Not *owe* me, but.

How much I *helped* you.

*Pause.*

JASON. Owe you? What do you want from me?

ALEX. Nothing!

JASON. Why have you come here?

ALEX. Well, why do you think I came here?

JASON. I thought you wanted to see the house.

ALEX. Come on

JASON. Obviously, I'm not completely naive, when you said
could you come and see the house, I'm not, I could have said
no

ALEX. We're at a *reunion.*

JASON. Yeh but I didn't know you'd held on to all these –

ALEX. I was kind to you, wasn't I? I was discreet – I never told
anyone about the, *difficulties*, you had,

JASON. Seriously, *difficulties*? You're making out it was
some big –

ALEX. I even listened to you talk about other girls, helped you
get together with –

JASON. Are you *sure* you haven't got me mixed up with someone else?

ALEX. Are you serious?

JASON. I just don't remember being like that

ALEX. Obviously you weren't like that on the *outside*. No one, your mates would never have imagined –

You were like you are now. All the chat – laddy lad. I gave you the confidence to catch up with yourself. The image you projected. I gave you the confidence I had.

Because I was a very confident person at that time.

JASON. Yeah, no I remember!

*Pause.*

ALEX. Look, nevermind.

*Pause.*

JASON (*laughs*). Sorry, I don't know what you want me to say.

ALEX. I don't know either

JASON. Y'know, what do you *want*? You want me to *thank* you? Yeah? For, I don't know, being, I don't know –

ALEX. Look.

Shit.

Can we just finish the wine, how did we get on to the whole milkshake-sperm story, I shouldn't have brought it up!

ALEX *laughs,* JASON *doesn't.*

I don't know why I said any of that.

ALEX *pours more wine in each of their glasses.*

JASON. You know, this is.

It's embarrassing, for me.

ALEX. Let's rewind, can we? Just forget the last five minutes. Go back to –

JASON. You crying for no reason?

ALEX. No, before that.

This evening's going well, isn't it?

JASON. You know, how far do you want us to go back?

ALEX (*laughs*). Thirty years?

*The door from the hall into the room opens and a nineteen-year-old girl is standing there. The bottom of her T-shirt is wrapped round her thumb and it's soaked in blood.*

JASON *and* ALEX *jump out of their skins.*

*This girl is* ALANNAH.

ALANNAH. Hi.

JASON. What the fuck?

ALEX. Shit!

ALANNAH. I'm not supposed to be here, obviously, I'm embarrassed, I was going to hide and then leave when you left / but you're not leaving, so.

JASON. Where have you come from? / What are you *doing*?

ALEX. Shit.

ALANNAH. The only toilet's through the kitchen. You probably know that, are you the new tenants? I realised I wasn't going to be able to hide all night, / I've come down.

JASON. Who the fuck are you?

ALANNAH. I used to live here. There's been this whole mess-up about my new house.

ALEX. There's blood, you're bleeding –

ALANNAH. I caught my thumb on the edge of the bed frame yep, I was trying to hide under the bed, it was a ridiculous –

JASON. What are you *doing* here?

ALEX. The ghost!

ALANNAH. Are you the new tenants?

JASON. I'm the owner.

ALANNAH. Oh!

JASON. You were supposed to have moved out in August.

ALANNAH. I did!

> ALANNAH *throws a look at* ALEX, *stares at her for a moment, something shifts in her.*

JASON. What are you doing here three months after you were supposed to have moved out?

ALANNAH. No, I did move out, I haven't been here the whole time! I'm just here for tonight. Because, I thought, because no one had moved in yet.

JASON. I'm selling it. The house is on the market. There's no way you should be here.

ALANNAH. I'm not here. I'm sub-letting a friend's room while she's in France for a year, I just needed to stay here tonight basically, until I can get in touch with my friend's housemate who's away for the weekend in Nottingham which I didn't know about and she didn't cut me a key yet, but she's coming back tomorrow night.

JASON. Okay, so I'm not interested in any of that. How did you get in? Did you hold on to a key? You haven't smashed a window or anything?

ALANNAH. I didn't *smash* it.

JASON. How did you get in?

ALANNAH. I *forced* a window /

JASON. I don't believe / this

ALANNAH. It only cracked a bit at the bottom, I don't mind giving you the money for that.

JASON. Which window?

ALANNAH. The small one in the bathroom.

JASON. For fuck's sake

JASON *leaves the room.*

ALANNAH *doesn't say anything.*

ALEX. Do you not have anywhere else you could go tonight?

ALANNAH. Not really no.

ALEX *nods. Makes a face, 'Shit!'*

*They wait in silence for a moment.*

ALANNAH. Hello, Raya. It's me.

ALEX. Sorry?

ALANNAH. It's me, Alannah. I really appreciate how you, thank you so much. It was kind of you to write to me. At that time. It was probably hard for you and. Thank you, your emails were – I saved them. I re-read them sometimes actually, if I'm having a bad day.

ALEX *looks at* ALANNAH *in confused panic.*

ALEX. What?

ALANNAH. Don't worry, I'm not going to say anything in front of him. Y'know I just. Hope everything is better. And. Thank you for all your support and kindness to me.

JASON *re-enters*

JASON. It's cracked – it needs new glass.

ALANNAH. I said I'll pay for it if you want.

JASON. It's not about paying for it, it's about organising someone to be here for the glazier /

ALANNAH. I can do that, I can be here

JASON. God's sake, you can't just break into houses you used to live in, / I could call the police

ALANNAH. I didn't break in!

JASON. You literally broke in!

ALANNAH. Okay sorry! / I feel bad about it!

JASON. I really don't need this /

ALANNAH. Chuck me out on the street then, if you want, but.

JASON. I'm obviously not going to chuck you out in the middle of the night, you know I'm not going to do that –

ALANNAH. Thank you so much. / Thank you.

JASON. You can stay here tonight but first thing in the morning, you're out.

ALANNAH. Of course, before first thing, I'm gone. Thank you. Thank you so much. / Thank you.

JASON. Alright.

ALANNAH. I need to get  something, for my bleeding, for my thumb.

ALANNAH *exits*.

JASON. I can't stay the night in a house on my own with a teenage girl.

ALEX. She's really weird.

JASON. I'm serious, I can't.

ALEX. Well, you've said she can stay now.

JASON. Listen. Can we swap?

Can I take the hotel room, and you stay here? I brought bedding, it's in my car, I can make the bed up for you quickly now. / I'll pay for the hotel.

ALEX. Oh I don't know

JASON. I wouldn't feel comfortable staying here on my own with a young girl

ALEX. It was such a shock when she appeared at the door.

JASON. So we swap, yeh? Are you okay to stay here?

ALEX. I can make a bed here, you don't need to give up your bed.

JASON. No, you have the bed, I'll just buy the hotel room off you.

ALEX. No, I don't want to do that.

JASON. Don't you? Okay. Why not?

ALEX (*laughs*). Well, this is awkward.

JASON. I think it makes more sense.

ALEX. So. You can't buy my hotel room off me –

JASON. I've got cash, I can give you the cash /

ALEX. Because I haven't booked a hotel.

JASON. Oh.

I thought you had.

ALEX *looks at* JASON *but doesn't say anything.*

You said you had a hotel.

ALEX *looks at him.*

I'm completely confused now, where were you going to stay?

ALEX. I don't know, Jason, I don't know.

JASON. You were just about to order a cab.

Where were you going to get a cab to?

ALEX. I don't know. I thought maybe I wouldn't need a hotel.

I thought something might happen.

ALANNAH *comes into the doorway holding a first-aid box and a plaster wrapped in a packet.*

ALANNAH. Can I use one of these plasters please?

JASON. Yeh, go ahead –

ALANNAH (*to* ALEX). Please can you get this plaster out of the packet? You need two hands

*The three of them stand in silence as* ALEX *takes the plaster out.*

It's not deep. So it's going to be fine.

*She takes the plaster from* ALEX *and wraps it round her thumb.*

All better.

So yeah, I've got a place sorted from tomorrow, it's just a mess-up about tonight.

JASON. Which room are you in?

ALANNAH. My things are in the back room but I can move, I've only got one bag.

JASON. It's okay stay where you are.

ALANNAH. Okay. Thank you.

(*To* ALEX.) Thank you.

Goodnight.

Sorry I'm here.

Night.

ALEX. Goodnight.

ALANNAH *goes out and upstairs.*

JASON. She thinks you're my wife.

ALEX. Of course she does.

Raya.

JASON. She dealt with all the contracts.

ALEX. Should I have said, told her that I'm not?

JASON *shakes his head.*

JASON. Doesn't matter.

ALEX *sits down on the edge of the chair, gets out her phone. Business-like.*

ALEX. So, yes. I don't have a hotel booked I'm afraid. But I can probably find a room, if I have a scout around

JASON. It's one in the morning

JASON *gets the car keys from his coat pocket.*

ALEX. There'll be something

JASON. You take the bed upstairs – I'll sleep down here.

ALEX. No that's crazy, that's not fair.

JASON. It's fine.

JASON *opens the front door and exits.*

ALEX. Let me at least –

ALEX *is by herself in the house, the front door open onto the night.*

*She sits stock still until* JASON *returns. She is remembering being here and being twenty and realising that in all disappointing likelihood, she must also have been foolish then.*

JASON *returns with bedding.*

ALEX *stands.*

Jason. I'm sorry. Can we.

JASON. Look, whatever, I'm easy, I don't care where I sleep.

ALEX. I'd rather you had the bed.

JASON. Okay, well let me just –

ALEX. I can do it –

*She watches while* JASON *unrolls a chair bed, puts some cushions down, lays a sheet over it.*

You just wanted the place to yourself and you've ended up with two strays.

JASON. It's fine.

ALEX. I'm an idiot. I'm a fantasist.

JASON. Don't worry about it.

ALEX. Oh no, we're strangers now.

JASON *finishes putting the sheet on.*

Hey – how about we finish the wine?

JASON. I'm gonna crash actually.

My daughter's at my in-laws tonight, she's being dropped off at ten and, we'll have to leave for London straight after that.

She's got a ballet exam.

ALEX. Right well, I'll definitely be gone by ten. Up early and, head back.

ALEX's *phone rings.*

*She rejects the call.*

JASON. Answer it, go ahead.

ALEX. I'd rather not end the evening like this.

JASON. Leave it. It's too weird and it's too late and –

ALEX. It's not too late!

JASON. I mean it's too late at night, I've been up since five thirty, I'm shattered.

ALEX. I don't want you to hate me.

JASON. I don't hate you.

ALEX. Shall we talk in the morning, go for breakfast

JASON. My daughter's being dropped off at ten.

ALEX. The ballet exam.

ALEX's *phone rings again.*

JASON. Answer it. I'm done, we're good.

JASON *hands* ALEX *a blanket. He waves. He leaves the room, closes the door.*

ALEX *sits on the edge of the bed.*

*After a moment she takes the call.*

ALEX. Hey.

Good thanks yeh, how are you?

Yeh it was good, weird seeing everyone, but fun. Interesting.

Are you at home?

Is Charlie there?

Did he eat?

That's good. Did he speak?

Well, did he *say* anything?

Has the date for the hearing come through?

Well, it's Sunday tomorrow.

They said they would but maybe we should call them.

I'm back at my hotel.

It's okay. Nothing particularly, nothing much to say about it. Just basic hotel kind of vibe.

I will yeah.

About three-ish.

I don't know, I haven't thought about it, maybe just mooch around the city a bit. Or smash my face into the plate glass window of a department store.

Or gouge my aged eyes out of my head with a rusty screwdriver, step off the kerb in front of a single decker bus.

Am I?

Can you hear me now?

Okay.

ALEX *stands and moves towards the window, as she approaches it the window disappears.* ALEX *moves beyond it.*

What about now, can you hear me now?

ALEX *moves towards the door, as she approaches it disappears.*

Now?

Can you hear me now?

*Darkness falls around her.*

Can you hear me now?

ALEX*'s voice continues in the dark.*

What about now? Hello?

Where is this?

My voice got unattached.

Have I rung myself from my bag.

So.

I came to a city and now I am at a house.

Hello *you*!

That's right.

There are cracks of light in the floor. Maybe there's a man in the cellar with a torch.

Root, root yourself. You spent the evening with familiar and now, hey presto, it's the gap between two places.

Guys, this is a ghost story! I'm scaring myself!

That's nothing to be frightened of.

*Light from a torch.*

ALANNAH *standing over* ALEX.

ALANNAH. Raya?

*Nothing.*

Raya?

*Nothing.*

*Then suddenly.*

ALEX. Yes?

ALEX *sits up*.

ALANNAH. Hello!

ALEX. Are you okay? / What's the matter?

ALANNAH. I need to tell you something /

ALEX. What time is it?

ALANNAH. The clocks either go back or forward tonight, what time does that happen, is it two?

ALEX. Two?

ALANNAH. But I don't know if that's old two or new two. So maybe it's one?

ALEX. Still?

ALANNAH. It's the one where you get an extra hour in bed so.

ALEX. Yes the clocks go back.

ALANNAH. So, how mad is it that you're here and I'm here on this one night? It's more than just a coincidence, do you think?

ALEX. Listen –

ALANNAH. This is so surreal, this is where I'd sit, here on the sofa emailing you. Can I turn the light on?

ALEX. I don't think that light works.

ALANNAH *flicks the light switch and the main light comes on*.

Oh! It does.

ALANNAH. So – wait till you hear this – Earlier on, the woman who did my service wash asked me about my tattoo, she said, is that your birthday, and I said no, it's the date of my dad's death, and she was like, oh my god I'm so sorry, and normally I would definitely cry, when that's happened before I just cry straight away, but today I was, yeah, he

killed himself, but it's fine, it happened, more matter of fact.
Afterwards I was like, what's wrong with me? I'm like made
of metal or something, like a metal heart. I was on my own
on the back seat of the bus and I asked him, it sounds weird
but, I asked my dad to give me a sign that it was okay not to
be sad, *all* the time. I've been so sad – I've been carrying this
big heavy bag of sadness around with me *everywhere,* well,
*you* know, and I asked him out loud, Dad, give me a sign that
it's okay with you if I put down the bag sometimes.

Then. About two minutes after that, I got off the bus and I
was walking past the end of this street and I had this thought,
just a random, just dropped into my head – Who are the new
tenants in Mill Road? I walked to the house and the bins
were empty and the lids were off, and I looked in the window
and I could see all these pizza leaflets on the floor and empty
bookshelves and I thought, you know what, there's no one
living in this house… hmm I wonder… Because I forgot to
say, but I had nowhere to stay tonight at that point. It was like
my dad was guiding me towards a solution. So, next thing,
round the back, forced the window, got in, looked around,
tried to sleep, but – I could feel this *tension* in my head, like
a ticking, like a *message* trying to get through or something
and – then what happens? I hear voices. First I'm scared but
I need the loo and so I force myself to come down and…
*You're* here, in this house, random – perfect – here you are.
You're the sign. The sign my dad sent me.

ALEX. Gosh that's, wow.

ALANNAH. I don't know if you got my last email, did you?

ALEX. I did / I think –

ALANNAH. Oh don't worry I expect you've been really busy

ALEX. I probably did, I mean I must have done.

*Beat.*

ALANNAH. You're not, I pictured you completely differently
in my head, not gonna lie.

ALEX. Oh. Well. This is what I look like! (*Touches her hair.*)

ALANNAH *looks at* ALEX *for a moment.*

ALANNAH. I just thought –

ALANNAH *considers expressing something but doesn't.*

ALEX *is self-conscious – opens her eyes wide and shrugs her shoulders.*

Wow! This is so mad! It's mad meeting someone for the first time but you feel like you know them.

ALEX. Yes!

ALANNAH. Is it weird for you to meet me?

ALEX. Yes definitely.

ALANNAH. I thought maybe the reason you were still downstairs after Jason went to bed was so that I would come down and we could talk.

ALEX. Oh, no, I was just, sleeping downstairs –

ALANNAH. Oh! Sorry then.

ALEX. It's okay.

ALANNAH. I probably shouldn't have come down, if you're trying to sleep.

ALEX. I'm awake now. I like your tattoos.

ALANNAH. Thank you.

ALEX. That one's very intricate.

ALANNAH. This one? It's to cover a big mistake underneath.

And this one is to cover a mistake I got on *this* arm, there used to be these naff wings here – he made them into her flowing cape, I'm going to get all this coloured in.

ALEX. Clever

ALANNAH. I don't like this one any more, it's really childish, this is just one mistake on top of another, I'm going to get that whole area covered. I used to think oh, it's such a mess,

you can still see the shape of the one underneath! But then
I thought well, you'd never have had that image on the top
if you hadn't had the mistake underneath and that's quite a
good way of looking at it I think, and a good way to think
about life as well. That feels like the kind of thing you'd say!
It's so mad that I'm sitting here talking to you.

ALEX. Yes, it's mad.

ALANNAH. Did I tell you I set up a climate change action
committee?

ALEX. I don't think so. No

ALANNAH. Oh right, I set up a climate change action
committee called 100 Seconds 2, because of the one hundred
seconds to midnight thing – you know how we need one
hundred billion dollars to undo the damage to the planet, and
the five hundred wealthiest people in the world have five
point three trillion dollars between them, well, we basically
meet twice a week and write to the five hundred people with
all the money to try and guilt-trip them into saving the earth.
We're bombarding them with emails, we spell it out for
them really clearly. One hundred billion dollars a year is
all it would take to turn back time! You've got five point
three *trillion*!

ALEX. That sounds like a, good for you!

ALANNAH. Only downside is, I've missed the last couple
of weeks of my Tuesday group, I need to get back to that.
Because –

ALANNAH *stands up*.

My favourite thing you ever said to me is, well, it's my
favourite thing ever really –

*She pulls down her leggings on one side to show* ALEX *a
tattoo on her thigh.*

'grief lurks around corners'.

Also it's obviously important to be part of the group for
new members.

ALEX *nods and smiles,* ALANNAH *expects that she might say something but* ALEX *doesn't know what to say.*

I got a different job! You know I was answering the phone in that property management office and all the men put their dirty coffee cups on my desk? Well. I got a job in a garden centre and I *love it*! It's so much more me – I look after all the outside plants and I'm close to nature and the couple who run it bring in flapjacks for everyone and give us cuttings. You told me to get a plant! I've got loads of plants! You were so right, it's a good way of focusing on time moving forwards. Unless they die! Which they haven't yet, so fingers crossed!

ALEX. Fingers crossed!

ALANNAH. Also, me and Miranda got back together.

ALEX. / Great!

ALANNAH. I know you're probably thinking *what*? What is she *doing*? But it's okay, we're in a much better place now, we've had lots of good talks. She accidently saw a text on my phone from my cousin calling her Mindbender, 'what's this about you getting back with Mindbender?' She was really upset. She said sorry about all that stuff, and actually I don't think she was gaslighting me. I think I was just freaked out because of her family's response to me, and I was in a fragile place because of my dad and I blew it all out of proportion. It was definitely fifty-fifty my fault as well. She is right, I am quite an oversensitive person. We are definitely in a much more mature relationship now.

Phew! I'm talking non-stop like I'm writing an email!

*She blows a kiss.*

Send!

ALEX *mimes being hit with a load of stuff in her face.*

ALEX. Delete! Delete!

ALANNAH *half-laughs.*

ALANNAH. Sorry!

ALEX. I'm joking!

*Pause.*

ALANNAH. What about *you*?

ALEX. / Good!

ALANNAH. How's life?

ALEX. Great!

ALANNAH (*beat*). Really?

ALEX. Yes. My son's back living at home but apart from that –

ALANNAH. Wait, you have a son? I thought you had two daughters.

ALEX. Yes, I have a son. As well.

ALANNAH. What! I didn't know you had a son! I'm so confused, how old's your son?

ALEX. He's twenty.

ALANNAH. And he lives with you?

ALEX. At the moment, but he's really at university / – in Leeds.

ALANNAH. Where? Oh in Leeds that's good.

ALEX. Leeds. Yes.

ALANNAH. My friend's at Leeds.

ALEX. Really?

ALANNAH. Yes. Doing Chemistry.

ALEX. Okay.

*Beat.*

ALANNAH. What's your son studying?

ALEX. Computer Science.

ALANNAH. What year is he in?

ALEX. He's just started his third year.

ALANNAH. My friend's in the third year! I wonder if they –

ALEX. It's a big place

ALANNAH. My friend's called Bailey, so that's / quite
an unusual,

ALEX. Right.

ALANNAH. Ask him if he knows a girl called Bailey.

ALEX. I don't think he does, well, you never know!

*Pause.*

ALANNAH. She's got her hair shaved, at the sides, here.

ALANNAH *hovers then commits and sits down on the arm
of the chair.*

I'll ask her, if she knows him

ALEX. Well he's actually at home at the moment so

ALANNAH. Oh, is he ill, or –

ALEX. No, he's –

ALANNAH. Oh my god I'm so nosy!

*Pause.*

I didn't know you had a son.

ALEX. I do. Yes. Charlie.

ALANNAH. I had worried when you stopped writing to me,
when you didn't answer my last email, I worried that maybe
I had written the wrong thing or that something bad had
happened, I expect it was just that you were busy, with
Charlie, was that it? Why you ignored my –

ALEX. I think so –

ALANNAH. How are Ella and Grace?

ALEX. Yes, everything's a bit – all-consuming

ALANNAH. How's Jason?

ALEX. He's great

ALANNAH. Oh, wow, / that's

ALEX. He's been looking after the girls and everything else

ALANNAH. Oh right. But. He had to stop work. Didn't he.

ALEX. That's right, he sold his share of the company, so that he could spend more time with us, so that's totally fine.

ALANNAH. Oh! Okay. So he's –

ALEX. He's still on the board, he travels all over the world, he's very involved in charities, he's on committees, he took a group of young care leavers to Cambodia to set up a football academy and he's very involved with a mental health, thing, he did a triathalon I think it was, to raise money for them – he set up a GoFundMe page – He's very busy. And supportive. Of everything.

ALANNAH. Right, – cos he did stop work, didn't he, after his breakdown.

ALEX. Oh right. Yeh.

ALANNAH. When he tried to – like my dad.

*Pause.*

ALEX. Well.

ALANNAH. Didn't he. At your holiday cottage…

*Pause.*

ALEX. I'm feeling pretty tired actually –

ALANNAH. In our emails.

ALEX. –

ALANNAH. Raya?

ALEX. I really am, so tired, I can't think straight.

ALANNAH. Oh. Okay.

ALEX. But's it's been so lovely to meet you, Elaine –

ALANNAH. Alannah

ALEX. Alannah, sorry, of course.

*Pause.*

ALANNAH. It's been lovely to meet you, too.

ALEX *nods*.

ALANNAH. I – sorry did I say the wrong thing?

ALEX. No, no, I just, we probably shouldn't talk about it.
While Jason's upstairs, you know. It's a bit. Private
and sensitive.

ALANNAH. Oh God of course, sorry.

*Pause.*

I probably told you things in my emails that I wouldn't have
said, if I'd known at the time that we were going to meet.
Is that how you feel as well?

ALEX. Yes, and it's, the middle of the night as well,
so – don't worry.

ALANNAH. I just came down and woke you up basically!

ALEX. Don't worry.

ALANNAH. I feel bad –

ALEX. No, no.

ALANNAH. Okay well, goodnight.

ALEX. Goodnight!

ALANNAH *hovers*.

ALANNAH. I haven't said anything about Jason, or what
happened in Suffolk, or the hospital. Just so you know. I
haven't told anyone about any of the things we talked about,
I promise you.

ALEX. Thank you.

ALANNAH. I haven't told Miranda. If you were worried about that.

ALEX. Okay – thanks.

ALANNAH. You probably think I'm so stupid, that stuff about my dad setting it up for me to meet you, as a sign!

ALEX. Not at all, no, I'm so sorry about your dad!

ALANNAH. Maybe there'll be another, a different sign, as well.

ALEX. Yes.

ALANNAH. I suppose it is still a *kind* of sign from my dad because we did have a bit of a conversation

ALEX. Yes we did.

I have to open a window or something, I'm having a hot flush sorry.

ALEX *jumps up and takes off a layer.*

Oh my goodness, this whole evening's been a car crash!

ALANNAH. You crashed your car?

ALEX. No, just tonight's been a disaster / everything's been so messed up

ALANNAH. Oh I thought you said you'd *had* a car crash

ALEX. I should have done, a head-on collision into a wall or something.

ALEX *fans her face and puts her hair up with a band from her bag. She sprays herself in the face and neck with an aerosol can with a bright-pink lid.* ALANNAH *watches her intently.*

That's better.

Okay.

ALANNAH. I'll go back upstairs, let you get some rest.

ALEX. No, don't go.

Would you like some of this wine?

ALANNAH. No I'm fine.

ALEX. How old are you, nineteen?

ALANNAH. Twenty.

ALEX. Twenty.

ALANNAH. Yes.

ALEX. Twenty's supposed to be when you have the best time, isn't it?

ALANNAH. Yeh, I don't know –

ALEX. It's a big pressure, and then things can just, derail, can't they?

ALANNAH. Yes

ALEX. Everything's just ticking along and then, in one moment –

ALANNAH. Everything stops.

ALEX. Charlie's not having the best time, I don't know maybe it was my responsibility, to make sure he understood things deep down, relationships you know

ALANNAH. Has he had a break-up? Is that why he's come home?

ALEX. Did your mother talk to you about things like that, it's easier with a girl perhaps – Maybe it's a mother-son thing – We're not entirely separate, are we, do you think? At your age? I don't know.

ALANNAH. I think I'm getting a thicker skin. I've been trying to do what you told me.

ALEX. Oh god don't listen to me!

ALANNAH *half-laughs*.

I was an idiot at twenty, not engaged with the world like you. I found my diaries, oh my god!

ALANNAH. I wrote a diary for about a week, but then it was just like, too sad. It was just like a long list of, sad.

ALEX. You should leave it, come back to it from further away.
I found it cathartic, reading it now, I had such a mixture of
emotions for myself, recognition, no recognition – revulsion,
shame, overprotective love for my young self. Perhaps that's
how we feel about our children.

Things aren't as you imagine they're going to be.

ALANNAH. Some people don't have a mind's eye, do they,
there's a girl in my Tuesday group who doesn't have one.

ALEX. A what?

ALANNAH. A mind's eye, she can't see images of things in
her imagination, things that she's seen happen – she can't
re-see them, and things that she's been told have happened
– she can't imagine them in pictures. Her mind is blind. I
don't know why I told you that! I just remembered it!
You've inspired me to write a diary now, I'm going to
start writing one.

ALEX. Yes so funny looking at old diaries!

The plans I made! My first love!

ALANNAH. I'm always scared someone would find it and
read it.

ALEX. His shoulders – in *my mind's eye* – in front of me in
the queue for the microfiche in the library, you won't know
what that is, there were machines and you used them like a
magnifying glass to look at tiny print on these huge sheets
of see-through plastic, if you wanted to research something,
it was a whole thing we had to do before the internet, I can't
describe it exactly. Anyway, each machine was labelled
Learner One, Learner Two, Learner Three, and you got given
a card, and he was on the Learner Two machine and I didn't
know his name so he was Learner Two. My friends would
be like 'there's Learner Two!', 'Learner Two's looking over
at you!' in the campus bar or wherever. He had a green and
orange bike and a sort of hessian bag, I would spot him. Get
myself in position, pretend not to notice him. Learner Two.

ALANNAH. You should have spoken to him.

ALEX. Yeh yeh. I did eventually. We'd meet up sometimes, at
the end of a night out. I'd come back to his.

*ALEX looks around the room.*

He met a local girl in a queue outside a club. Her parents ran
a pub and it had the same name as the pub his parents had
their first date in. The Three Bells. He thought it was fate.

(*Laughs.*) Wow how do I remember these things? I couldn't
tell you what happened in a film I watched two nights ago
but I remember all sorts of random –

*The light flickers and then goes out.*

*It makes* ALEX *and* ALANNAH *jump and they both
involuntarily give a small scream, then a laugh.*

Oh hang on, wait there's a lamp, / hold on

ALANNAH. I've got a torch / on my phone

ALEX. This light didn't work earlier / when

ALANNAH. Here –

*The light from the torch on* ALANNAH*'s phone lights a
section of the room,* ALEX *is fumbling to find the lamp.*

ALEX. When we first came in the house, there must be a dodgy
connection or something, where's the, here / here we are

*ALEX switches the lamp on.*

*JASON is standing in the room.*

*ALEX and* ALANNAH *are startled by him, they both
scream, laugh.*

JASON. What are you doing?

ALEX. What are *you* doing? / *Hanging* there, like a spectre

JASON. What time is it?

ALEX. Lurking around in the shadows / freaking us out!

ALANNAH. 2.34, so I / think that's

ALEX. Clocks go back, 1.34?

ALANNAH. 3.34?

JASON. Do I just pick one?

ALEX. There's definitely something wrong with the light!
Did we wake you up?

JASON. No, I don't sleep well anyway

ALEX. Are you okay? / Did you –

JASON. Yes I'm fine

ALEX. Oh good, you're okay – that's great.

*Pause.*

JASON. I came down to use the bathroom, so.

JASON *leaves the room.*

ALANNAH. I should go to bed.

ALEX. Okay well goodnight, good luck with everything.

ALANNAH. Raya. Will you come to my graduation?

ALEX. Oh!

ALANNAH. It's not for ages, but you get two tickets. I
wouldn't be having a graduation if you hadn't pulled me
through. You probably think that's overdramatic. I definitely
would have dropped out of university, you stopped me.

ALEX. Oh well I'm glad – /

ALANNAH. Everything went from normal to madness when
they found my dad.

I know what you're going to say, what's normal?
I don't know.

But when we were emailing, and you said I didn't have to
pay my rent. Oh my God. And the books, the one about
traumatic grieving, that's the best book I've ever read, it's

like the handbook to my life! Do you want them back by
the way? You never answered, if you give me your address
I can –

ALEX. It's fine /

ALANNAH. You were always awake, even when I emailed you
really late at night. And when you said I should ask for what
I needed – oh my god that thing you said about ending emails
with no worries if not! I've told *so* many people that, and
they're all like Oh My God! Every time I write an email now
I'm like, Do. Not. Write. That. You made me feel so much
more confident and able to cope with things.

It would be amazing if you could come to my graduation, on
my dad's ticket.

Of course I totally understand if you can't come.

ALEX. Oh I don't know.

ALANNAH. It might be at the same time as Charlie's
graduation. I hadn't thought about that, I didn't know you
had a son, is he going to finish his degree? / Probably he is,
so yeh.

ALEX. Hopefully.

ALANNAH *watches* ALEX.

ALEX *fans herself with her hand.*

ALANNAH. Are you having the menopause?

ALEX. It's a fucking nightmare!

ALANNAH. My mum is as well. She freaks out at the tiniest
thing, if she has to put a duvet cover on or something.
She's impossible.

ALEX. Just you wait. It will happen to you. You won't
recognise a single thought in your head, you'll cry all the
time, forget everything. It's exhausting.

You'll go from being a perfectly normal shape, to looking
like a toddler's made you out of playdough.

Enjoy oestrogen – when it runs out it's game over.

That's it. End of joy. I know you don't want to hear it but one day you'll find yourself older in a world that values youth and you'll look back and see how easy it was to be young.

ALANNAH. It's not that easy to be young.

ALEX. No, I know.

ALANNAH. And you can get HRT. / So...

ALEX. You can.

ALANNAH *hovers in the doorway.*

ALANNAH. Graduation's not for ages so. We can talk about it nearer the time. No pressure.

Is it all right if I hug you?

ALEX. I'm a bit sweaty.

ALANNAH *hugs* ALEX, *she holds her for a bit longer than* ALEX *expects.*

*They part.*

ALANNAH *goes upstairs.*

ALEX *waits.*

*Suddenly she quickly lies down and pulls the covers over her and lies still.*

*Then she changes her mind, gets up and sits, waiting.*

*It's very quiet in the house.*

ALEX *gets freaked by the quiet. She calls.*

Jason?

*Quiet house.* ALEX *calls again.*

Jase?

JASON *appears in the room.*

JASON. Hi.

ALEX. Hi!

JASON. What was the stowaway saying to you?

ALEX. Nothing really, just talking about being a student.
Are you okay?

JASON. Yes, I heard you talking, / I thought you were on
the phone.

ALEX. Could you hear what we were saying?

JASON. No. / Why, what were you saying?

ALEX. So, are you okay? / Nothing!

JASON. Yes. Sorry I ducked out.

ALEX. I should have booked somewhere, I shouldn't have
invited myself back here, I shouldn't have presumed.
So much I should have done differently! / Mortifying

JASON. Listen. Do you fancy –

ALEX. What?

JASON. I dunno, rewinding a bit –

ALEX. Yes. Yes. To earlier in the evening or –

JASON. It's up to you.

ALEX. Okay.

JASON. Further back if you like.

*Pause. More awkward than* JASON *expected.*

I thought that's what you wanted, / that's what you wanted –

ALEX. Yeh –

JASON. Have I got it wrong?

ALEX. No, no. It's just –

Are you, *okay*?

JASON (*pause*). Yeh.

Fine.

Why?

ALEX. Nothing, I just. Had a feeling that. I just wanted to check in, and make sure, that everything's okay that's all.

JASON. I'm good. I'm on board.

Are you?

ALEX. We don't have to do anything, we could just talk, I'd be fine with that.

JASON. No, what you said before, it was good. This doesn't have to be about any real-life stuff. Let's have an amnesty, this house is a time machine, we have one night of oblivion.

ALEX. What's that from?

JASON. Nowhere. My head.

ALEX. Not very you!

JASON. This isn't me, is it?

ALEX. Are you drunk?

JASON. No, I'm – not drunk.

*Pause, then* ALEX *stands. She steps towards* JASON.

*He laughs, looks away briefly.* ALEX *laughs.*

Okay!

*It seems as if* JASON *is forcing himself to look at her and stay focused.*

ALEX *can feel this, it's weird but she stays with it.*

ALEX *and* JASON *start to kiss.*

JASON *closes his eyes.*

ALEX *stops and steps back a bit.*

ALEX. Is this okay? You're okay with this?

JASON. I'm the one who came back downstairs –

ALEX. Okay, great. / Great!

JASON. Are *you* okay with it? Because, y'know. If –

ALEX *grabs a sip of her wine.*

ALEX. Dutch courage

JASON. Sit down

*They sit down next to each other.*

*They start to kiss.*

*It's tentative and clumsy and awkward. They focus on kissing.*

*Then stop kissing.*

ALEX. This feels weird, is this weird?

JASON. I don't know what it's supposed to feel like, I don't do this –

ALEX. Have you got a drink, where's your glass?

JASON. It's in the kitchen

ALEX *jumps up.*

I'll get it

JASON *lets her go.*

ALEX. I'm there!

ALEX *exits to the kitchen.*

JASON *puts his head deeply into his hands and sits very still.*

*After a few moments* ALEX *returns with two mugs,* JASON *rallies, sits upright.*

Let's do this properly

JASON. Not the mugs!

ALEX. It has to be done.

ALEX *pours wine into two mugs. She finishes the bottle.*

*They sit next to each other.*

*They clink mugs.*

JASON *rolls his eyes and shakes his head.*

*They drink.*

ALEX *starts to kiss* JASON. *She leans into him.*

ALEX *clambers on to his lap as they kiss. Gets a bit caught up in the bedding they are sitting on, she has to free her foot.*

*They kiss and* ALEX *starts to take off* JASON*'s T-shirt over his head. It's easier if he does it himself.* JASON *starts to do it and stops halfway through. He leans his head back.*

*They are still for a moment, and then* ALEX *gets off him and sits beside him.*

*Silence.*

JASON. Sorry.

ALEX. It feels a bit forced, doesn't it?

JASON. I'm not forcing you! / What?

ALEX. I mean, we're sort of pushing uphill to make it happen, do you think?

JASON. Maybe yeh.

ALEX. Let's. It's okay. There's no rush is there?

JASON *rubs his face with his hands.*

Thirty years ago, when we were sat here /

JASON. There was a sofa.

ALEX. And it was over there under the window, wasn't it?

JASON. There was an armchair there and a sofa, whatever –

ALEX. I was going to say – We had no sense of what looking back was going to feel like. We didn't imagine a moment when we might look back. It's our blind spot. You look back now and remember how it felt, or at least how you *think* you felt, even that's not totally reliable.

*Pause.*

What happens to all the moments that you can't remember, do they exist?

JASON. If a tree falls in a forest and no one's there to hear it...

ALEX. And if two people have completely different memories of the same event, what is the truth? What happens to fact? If no one can be sure of how it was.

What's left of the event?

Nothing?

A blank. A gap.

JASON. You threw me, bringing all that stuff up. / I *do* remember –

ALEX. It feels so long ago physically, bodily. I can't catch hold of it.

JASON. Cells regenerate every ten years or something don't they, we are completely new people

ALEX. So, we've never even actually met!

JASON. I *do* remember, you and me.

ALEX. Is that what you meant when you said you weren't you?

JASON. You don't know me. Any more. You don't really know anything about my life.

ALEX. We don't have to talk about it if you don't want to.

JASON. You were an important – remembering it now, I think I wrote you a letter in fact. / After everything.

ALEX. You did, yes.

JASON. Y'know, saying I appreciated, I dunno. What you were saying earlier.

ALEX. I've got it in my bag.

JASON (*laughs*). Yeh, exhibit A!

ALEX. No, I really have.

JASON. What, you're joking (*Laughs.*)

ALEX. I found it. When I was going through stuff.

*She gets her bag, she looks for the letter.*

JASON (*not laughing*). Are you serious? *What?*

*She finds the letter.*

ALEX. Here.

*She offers it to* JASON.

*He is appalled.*

JASON. I don't want to see it.

ALEX. Don't you want to read it?

JASON. No.

ALEX. It's a really sweet letter.

JASON. I really don't want to read it, no.

ALEX. Okay.

JASON. What are you going to do with it?

ALEX. Nothing. / What do you mean?

JASON. Why have you kept it for thirty years?

ALEX. Everyone keeps letters.

JASON. Why did you bring it with you?

ALEX. I thought you might want to read it, it's a piece of
personal history.

    ALEX *puts the letter back in her bag.*

You don't have to.

*She takes a miniature bottle of wine out of her bag.*

Oh look!

From the train!

*She opens the bottle and tops up their mugs.*

JASON. We're giants!

*They clink mugs.*

ALEX. To being middle-aged giants that have never met!

Better than young bodies, great sex?

JASON. Fractionally.

Definitely more realistic.

*They drink in silence.*

*Above them* ALANNAH *walks across the room, sound of her door closing.*

ALEX. I feel like a lot goes on under the surface with you, that you don't necessarily show, would you say that was fair?

JASON. I don't know.

ALEX. It's just something I'm picking up

JASON. Is this where you get the tarot cards out?

ALEX. You married a therapist you must speak the language.

JASON. Not fluently.

*Pause.*

Please, Alex, I just want a night off.

JASON *looks straight ahead.*

I'm fine!

ALEX. I went to a friend's fiftieth a couple of months ago, it was in a room above a pub, and when I got there I couldn't see anyone I knew. I got a drink and fell in talking to some people and they were nice and I relaxed into it. After twenty minutes or so I worked out that I literally didn't know a single person there, I'd got the day wrong, I was a week early! I was at a stranger's party! By then I'd had a couple of drinks so I just stayed. I had such a great night!

JASON. Okay.

ALEX. Random story for you there. About escaping yourself.

JASON. Is that what you're doing here?

ALEX. Is that what *I'm* doing here?

JASON. I don't know, I just wondered –

ALEX. I don't think I'm escaping myself. I think I'm looking for myself, I hoped I'd find myself hidden somewhere in this house.

Hang on, is that the same thing? When you're fifty, is escaping yourself just the flip side of finding yourself? Maybe it all joins up into a great big stupid futile circle.

What a detour this is, you're just a cul-de-sac.

JASON (*laughs*). Thanks a lot!

ALEX (*laughs*).

JASON. Fucking rude!

You're a bit of a cul-de-sac yourself!

ALEX (*laughs*).

JASON. Do you know what that means?

ALEX. Course I do.

JASON. What?

ALEX. A dead end, when you have to do a U-turn / to get out of

JASON. No, the literal translation,

ALEX. Street something? What is this, a pub quiz?

JASON. Yeh – it's your round. And get a bigger bottle this time.

ALEX. What is the literal translation then?

JASON. Arse of a bag.

ALEX. Arse?

JASON. Of a bag

ALEX. No it's not /

JASON. Cul. De. Sac. Arse of a bag.

ALEX *looks disbelieving*.

Look it up!

ALEX. I will!

*ALEX gets her phone from her bag. She stops when she sees the screen.*

Wait. Sorry.

*She stands up.*

I just have to –

JASON. What's the matter?

ALEX. I've just got a missed call from my son, thirteen minutes ago, it's so late! I need to call him back.

*ALEX is returning the call, it's ringing. ALEX turns her back and moves away from JASON*

Sorry, I just.

JASON. Go ahead.

*ALEX is waiting for her son to pick up.*

*JASON downs his wine and pours more into his mug from the tiny bottle. He looks towards ALEX and makes a mime about being a giant or needing a magnifying glass but she is not looking at him.*

*ALEX's son's phone goes to answer machine. ALEX hangs up without leaving a message.*

ALEX. It's the answer phone.

JASON. Leave a message.

ALEX. He won't listen to it.

JASON. He's asleep.

ALEX. It's weird that he called me.

JASON. Is he on his own in the house?

*ALEX calls again.*

*She is uneasy.*

ALEX. He never calls me.

*We hear the call go to answer phone again.*

Oh well.

ALEX *puts her phone down on the table.*

*All of a sudden* ALEX *rises, full of vehement, irrational resolve.*

I might go, I should go

JASON. What do you mean, / go where?

ALEX. What am I doing here it's ridiculous, I'm going home

JASON. To London? How? / You came on the train, didn't you?

ALEX. I'll get a cab

JASON. To London?

ALEX. I want to go home.

JASON. That's crazy!

ALEX. Could you give me the money for a cab please.

JASON. Are you serious? Your son's fine!

ALEX. What do *you* know? You said you had cash, how much cash have you got?

JASON. I mean, obviously if you need to.

ALEX. I need to go home, yeh

JASON. How old is your son, / I thought he was at university.

ALEX. Was there a girl here?

JASON. What?

ALEX. Just now, a girl. She forced the bathroom window and climbed in

JASON. *What?*

ALEX. She'd cut her thumb. There was blood

ALEX *is looking on the carpet for bloodstains.*

Did you see her? Was she here? / Was she?

JASON. Yes! Of course she was! You know she was.

ALEX. Okay good. That's okay. Good.

JASON. What do you *mean*?

ALEX. She was here. You saw her. I spoke to her. She's gone to bed.

*JASON stands.*

JASON. Are you okay?

ALEX. Yeh.

JASON. What's going on?

Are you going to get a cab back to London?

ALEX. Why does he do this, why can't he just answer his phone?

JASON. It would probably be about three hundred quid.

*ALEX tries calling Charlie again.*

*JASON gets his wallet and counts out some notes.*

*Charlie's phone goes to answer phone, ALEX puts the phone away in her bag.*

ALEX. Don't worry I'm just losing my mind.

JASON. I mean, I've got cash

*JASON holds the cash out to ALEX.*

ALEX. I don't know what happened exactly – he seems to be under investigation for – no one knows the exact circumstances – from what I can understand there was some incident. With a girl.

JASON. What sort of incident?

ALEX. I haven't quite got to the bottom of it yet. It's difficult to piece it all together through a closed door. I'm not trying to defend him – she's incredibly upset about it – he had to come home.

JASON. Oh okay.

ALEX. She had said yes I think earlier on in the evening, and then changed her mind. And said No.

*Pause.*

JASON *offers the cash.* ALEX *declines it.*

It's fine, don't worry.

JASON. I'd happily – if you need to

ALEX. It's fine.

JASON. Why don't you ring your husband if you're worried.

ALEX. He blames me, I blame him, so that's a bit of a stuck record. Anyway he'll be busy thinking about a woman he works with.

JASON. What do you mean?

ALEX. He thinks about her all the time.

JASON. How do you know?

ALEX. I just know. He gives her lifts, he drives miles out of his way. One night I said to him, you're late! He said, yes, I gave this plain Jane a lift home. Plain Jane! Who calls someone a plain Jane unless they're trying to put you off the scent. It all fell into place – the new music he'd been downloading, all these young artists. Gifs.

I became the dunce overnight. Our whole house turned against me, the effort I'd put into it, the things I'd chosen – candles, cups, the photos I'd framed – all mocking me.

I can't be at home. I'm drab in all the mirrors. I've spent twenty-five years trailing around after my husband on a tour of his life.

JASON. What happened?

ALEX. When?

JASON. With him and Jane.

ALEX. She's not called Jane, she's called, wait for it, Salome.

No nothing's *happened,* he wouldn't be able to live with
himself if it had. It's worse than that. It's just slump.
It's just sagging.

We've exhausted each other, after all the time that's gathered,
we can't see past the inside of each other's heads. Ageing
together's a slow drift into complacency and acceptance.

It started before Salome, when he stopped recognising me in
public places – it happened once and then it happened again
– I was walking towards him smiling, waving, saying his
name and he didn't *see* me. Or he did see me but didn't know
it was me, something strange and new. I'd stopped being
someone who existed out in the world.

Then my son came home.

I don't sleep. My husband's head is full of her, next to mine
on the pillow, maybe if he'd spent more time talking to his
son rather than – and Charlie's pacing on the other side of
the wall, and I can't fix it for him, and all three of us choking
in a house that's filling up with private thoughts, and mine
fester – and form a crust over everything – and I have to *do*
something, I have to *smash* it, otherwise

ALEX *stops.*

JASON. How are you going to smash it?

ALEX. I don't know. Have sex with you?

JASON. Really?

ALEX. Except I can't even get that right.

*Pause.*

Ignore me. I don't know why I'm trying to make this impact
on you – It's not fair. You were minding your own business
and then along comes me on my futile journey, you're just a
stop on the way.

Go back to bed, forget tonight. I'll be gone in the morning,
I promise.

Then you can go back to your girls, and your wife, and I'll just fade back into a list of Facebook friends you crossed paths with once.

*The sound of* ALANNAH's *footsteps as she crosses the room above them.*

JASON. You should leave him.

ALEX. For thinking about someone? / Is that allowed?

JASON. If you're not happy. It's a waste of time.

ALEX. How do I know if I'm not happy? / How do I measure it?

JASON. It's pretty obvious

ALEX. Three out of five stars, two out of five?

JASON. Cut your losses.

ALEX. Thank you that's. I hope your wife's therapy skills are more finely tuned than yours.

JASON (*makes a face*). I'm just saying, what's the point?

ALEX. Yep. You don't know anything about it so, thanks, but.

*Pause.*

JASON. Fair enough.

ALEX. Now what? How did we get here?

JASON. Where were we?

ALEX. We were at a reunion, we came back to a house.

JASON. Do you want to come upstairs?

ALEX. I need to work out what I'm doing.

JASON. Do you want to come upstairs after that?

ALEX. I don't know.

I'd forgotten how steep those stairs are.

JASON. It's okay if you want to call it a day.

ALEX. Do you ever feel like you've grown out of your own personality?

JASON. No

ALEX. I feel out of my depth. I can't get a foothold.

JASON. There are worse things.

ALEX. What do you mean?

JASON. Worse things happen.

ALEX. I know! What are you saying?

JASON. You do have quite a negative outlook on life.

ALEX. No I don't.

JASON. The photos of dead garage flowers – /

ALEX. That's an art project, are you mocking me?

JASON. No it's just all a bit bleak. Freaking out about your son.

ALEX. At least I engage emotionally with what's going on around me, at least I *feel* things.

JASON. I feel things.

ALEX. You don't express them /

JASON. How do you know, you haven't set eyes on me for thirty years /

ALEX. I want to go to sleep now, down here.

JASON. Go ahead!

ALEX. You're sitting on my bed

JASON. Okay.

    JASON *stands up*.

ALEX. I shouldn't have come back here, I don't know who I thought I would be here, I'm not anyone.

JASON. I'm sorry if I offended you /

ALEX. My head feels numb, I'm not anyone.

JASON. You're tired, I'm tired

ALEX. I'm just someone who's embarrassed about all the things that have happened.

JASON. No worries, shall I turn this light off for you?

ALEX. I bet you're a lovely dad

JASON. I'm not going to sing to you if that's what you're after.

ALEX. That is a really Dad thing to say

JASON *laughs*.

ALEX *sprays herself in the face and neck with her aerosol and gets into bed. She throws off the bedding.*

In my defence can I just say that research has shown that a reduction of oestrogen can potentially trigger or aggravate mental disorders including psychosis /

JASON. That's your defence?

ALEX. Oestrogen is the chair that God pulls away just as a woman is about to sit down! Not God, nature! Men!

JASON. Men? Don't try and pin it on me, I never pulled away your oestrogen chair.

ALEX. There are thirty-four symptoms associated with the fucking menopause, thirty-four! Can you imagine if men got something that had thirty-four symptoms? You'd be up in arms! They'd spend *millions* on fixing it. Thirty-four symptoms. It's an *ambush*. Of course I can't remember what any of them are so – don't ask me.

JASON *switches off the lamp*.

Goodnight, Jason.

JASON. Night, Ray.

*Pause*.

I'm sorry. Goodnight, Alex.

*Sound of the door closing in the dark.*

*Silence.*

*Darkness.*

*Whispering softly indecipherable at first.*

*Then:*

ALEX (*whispered*). Why didn't you answer?

You called *me*. I thought something was wrong.

Is something wrong?

Okay sorry go back to sleep then.

What did you ring me for?

Oh. Okay

Did you find it?

Was it on the hook by the – Yeh.

Okay.

Because I'm in a house I used to stay in when I was a student and I'm trying not to wake anyone up.

Just some other people that used to be students.

Charlie.

Charlie, do you want to talk for a bit?

Are you still there?

Is Dad in?

Are you still there?

*Darkness.*

Are you still there, Charlie?

Are you?

Charlie? Are you there?

*Silence as the light slowly comes up on…*

*Morning.*

*The walls and door have moved back into the shape of the room.*

*There are voices in the kitchen talking and laughing, it is* ALANNAH *talking to* JASON.

*A mobile phone rings in the kitchen, we hear* JASON *answer it.*

ALEX *wakes.*

*Her memory serves up the elements of the night before.*

JASON *walks through to the front door with his phone in his hand.*

JASON (*to* ALEX). My daughter's here. She's being dropped off now, Gran and bloody Grandpa forgot the clocks went back, what time is it, / is it five past nine?

ALEX *scrabbles around to find her phone.*

God's sake. Hopefully they won't come in, they'll think I've turned into Peter Stringfellow.

Alex, can you –

JASON *exits out of the front door.*

ALANNAH *comes in with a cup of tea.*

ALEX *sits up.*

ALEX. Oh.

ALANNAH. Did you sleep well?

ALEX. Not bad. You?

ALEX *is sheepish, not quite able to look at* ALANNAH, *does she still believe she is Raya? Looking for signs.*

ALANNAH. Deeply. This house has good vibes.

I went to the shop and got tea and milk and bread, I crept past you, you were fast asleep. I forgot margarine though. Do you want some dry toast?

ALEX. No I'm fine thanks.

Thank you for the tea.

ALEX *stands up, she starts to fold up the bedding.*

ALANNAH. Thanks for pretending to be Raya by the way.

ALEX *stops what she's doing.*

ALEX. Oh my god, you *know*, how do you *know*?

ALANNAH. I was talking to Jason in the kitchen, he said you were friends at college.

ALEX. Okay. I'm so sorry, I tripped into it, it was bad –

ALANNAH. No, I'm relieved, you were weird! You were so different from what I expected Raya to be like, I knew something was wrong. Everything about you was wrong! When you said delete when I pretended to send an email –

ALEX. I was joking, that was a joke

ALANNAH. I know, it just isn't the kind of joke Raya would make.

ALEX. I think she's much nicer than me.

ALANNAH. No, you're nice as well. It was nice of you to pretend, you probably thought I needed you to be her, did you?

*A ten-year-old girl comes through the front door and into the room. She is immaculately dressed for a ballet exam, leotard, tights, hair scraped perfectly into a bun. Trainers instead of ballet shoes.*

*She is* GRACE.

*She stands by the door.*

ALEX. Oh hi! / Hello. Are you Grace? I'm Alex.

ALANNAH. Hey, Grace, I'm Alannah

ALEX. You look amazing! / Wow! Look at you!

ALANNAH. So cool, I love your leotard.

ALEX. You've got a ballet exam, haven't you? So exciting, are you nervous?

GRACE *doesn't say anything she just stares at them.*

I used to do ballet when I was your age, but I wasn't very good. I think I only did one exam, we had to do a dance with ribbons I remember.

*Pause.*

Do you have to do a dance with ribbons?

GRACE *shakes her head.*

ALEX *turns to* ALANNAH.

Did you do ballet?

ALANNAH. No I didn't actually. No.

*They stand in silence for a moment.*

*Then* ALANNAH *takes a folded piece of paper out of her back pocket and moves towards* GRACE *and holds it out to her.*

Grace, would you mind, please would you give this letter to your mummy for me?

GRACE *stares at her.*

Would that be okay?

*After a moment* GRACE *tentatively takes the letter.*

ALANNAH *steps back.*

Thank you I appreciate that.

*The three of them stand in awkward silence for a moment or two.*

GRACE *holds the letter.*

ALEX *starts to get her stuff together.*

ALEX. Are you going to be able to move into your room today?

ALANNAH. Yeh yeh that's all cool, my friend's boyfriend's giving me his key so.

Jason said he'd give me a lift actually. Which is really kind of him. I could get the bus but he said he's driving out that way – So I'm going to come in the car with you, Grace! If that's okay.

GRACE *looks away.*

JASON *comes back into the house.*

JASON. Hey!

(*To* GRACE.) So Gran and Grandpa didn't remember the clocks went back! They'd have opened the pub an hour early. Did you forget as well?

GRACE *shows* JASON *the letter in her hand.*

What's this?

JASON *takes the letter and looks at it.* GRACE *is searching his face.*

Oh! Okay. That's okay. No problem.

JASON *puts his hand on* GRACE's *back and turns to face* ALEX *and* ALANNAH

So, unfortunately.

Sadly.

We can't give this note to Raya, because Raya died.

ALANNAH *gasps. Steps back towards* ALEX.

Is this, what's this, who's this from?

ALANNAH. Me, it was just –

JASON. That's okay, yeh. Raya died three-and-a-half months ago, in a hospice, so.

She's no longer with us I'm afraid

which is desperate,

umm, it's desperately sad,

it's unthinkable really.

but

we are trying our best. To move forwards.

Gradually.

Onwards and upwards.

(*To* GRACE.) Aren't we?

(*To* ALANNAH.) Shall I give this back to you? Yes.

JASON *hands the letter back to* ALANNAH, *she takes it, doesn't know what to do with it, holds it uselessly.*

ALEX. I'm so sorry, Jason. / So sorry.

ALANNAH. I'm really sorry For your loss.

JASON. Thank you. Yes, thank you.

(*Checking in with* GRACE.) So it's just the three of us now, isn't it? The A Team. We're not doing too badly, are we?

And we are going to absolutely nail this ballet exam, aren't we?

There's no talking or laughing apparently /

GRACE (*to* JASON). You lose marks if you talk or laugh

JASON. Oh my God, are you serious? *Lose marks*?

ALEX. That's very strict, isn't it?

JASON. So strict.

(*To* GRACE.) Right, did you go to the loo?

GRACE. No.

JASON. Go on then, hurry up, it's through the kitchen.

GRACE *runs through and out the room.*

Right.

ALEX *tries to make contact with* JASON *but he is not contactable.*

So. I'm giving you a lift.

ALANNAH. I can really easily get a bus.

JASON. No, no that's fine. Where's your bags? Bring them down and I'll put them in the car.

ALANNAH *leaves the room, as she goes she makes eye contact with* ALEX, *she still has the folded note in her hand.*

*She considers giving it to* ALEX, *doesn't, then goes upstairs.*

ALEX. Why didn't you say?

JASON. I just wanted one night off I told you.

ALEX. You could have talked to me about it, / I would have –

JASON. I didn't want to. Thanks.

ALEX. So you organised a party where you wouldn't know anyone.

*Pause.*

JASON. I wanted to see if it was possible to forget for an hour or –

ALEX. Was it? / No

JASON. No of course not.

*Pause.*

ALEX. She was obviously a really lovely person /

JASON. Yup

ALEX. She was extraordinarily kind to Alannah, her father killed himself, did you know that? Raya wrote to her and made a huge difference, supported her, held her, / really went the extra mile

JASON. I can't get into this, now. That's sad, obviously, but –

ALEX. Let's meet up, like you said, in London yes?

JASON. Don't worry about it, you weren't looking for that, /
you were looking for something else, that's fine.

ALEX. I was! I want to! Of course I do

JASON. I'm sorry I couldn't offer you what you wanted, but –

ALEX. I wish we could start the night again /

JASON. You can't go back, if there's one thing I understand
now it's that.

What you had is what you had and that's it.

GRACE *comes back into the room.*

Okay?

GRACE. The floors in this house are really good for ballet.

JASON. Oh really? Are they not slippy?

GRACE. They're sort of bouncy.

JASON (*nods, interested*). Bouncy floors, good.

GRACE *does a plié.*

GRACE *does a tendu.*

GRACE. I can't do it properly in trainers.

JASON. Mind out you're right in front of the door.

GRACE *moves to the other side of the room.*

ALANNAH *comes down with her bag.*

Let me take that.

ALANNAH. No, it's heavy.

JASON. I'll take it it's fine.

ALANNAH *gives JASON her bag.*

JASON *takes it and goes out to the car.*

*As soon as he leaves* ALEX *goes to* ALANNAH.

ALEX. I didn't know that, I one hundred per cent did not know
that, do you hear me?

ALANNAH (*nods*). Okay

ALEX. I would *never*, if I had known.

> ALANNAH *nods*.

> Are you okay?

> ALANNAH *nods*.

> ALEX *gathers up the mugs and takes them into the kitchen.*

> GRACE *does a plié.* ALANNAH *watches her.*

ALANNAH. You're good.

GRACE. I can't do it properly in trainers.

ALANNAH. Take them off!

> GRACE *takes her trainers off straight away. So does*
> ALANNAH.

> GRACE *does a plié.* ALANNAH *copies her.*

> ALEX *comes back in from the kitchen.*

ALEX. Hey! Beautiful!

> ALEX *packs the last few things into her bag and watches*
> GRACE *and* ALANNAH.

> GRACE *does a tendu.* ALANNAH *copies her.*
> ALEX *laughs.*

ALANNAH. It's harder than it looks!

ALEX. You're good!

> ALEX *crosses the room to get her coat.*

> *En route she joins in with a plié.*

> *For a moment the three of them synchronise exactly and*
> *perfectly, then* ALEX *puts her coat on and the moment*
> *has passed.*

> *The End.*